YOUR KNOWLEDGE HAS VALUE

Michael A. Braun

Foreign direct investments in Poland since 1989 - Theoretical background, specific advantages and recent developments

GRIN Verlag

Bibliografische Information der Deutschen Nationalbibliothek:

Die Deutsche Bibliothek verzeichnet diese Publikation in der Deutschen National-
bibliografie; detaillierte bibliografische Daten sind im Internet über http://dnb.d-
nb.de/ abrufbar.

Imprint:

Copyright © 2003 GRIN Verlag GmbH
Druck und Bindung: Books on Demand GmbH, Norderstedt Germany
ISBN: 978-3-640-18424-8

This book at GRIN:

http://www.grin.com/en/e-book/69566/foreign-direct-investments-in-poland-since-
1989-theoretical-background

GRIN - Your knowledge has value

Der GRIN Verlag publiziert seit 1998 wissenschaftliche Arbeiten von Studenten, Hochschullehrern und anderen Akademikern als eBook und gedrucktes Buch. Die Verlagswebsite www.grin.com ist die ideale Plattform zur Veröffentlichung von Hausarbeiten, Abschlussarbeiten, wissenschaftlichen Aufsätzen, Dissertationen und Fachbüchern.

Visit us on the internet:

http://www.grin.com/

http://www.facebook.com/grincom

http://www.twitter.com/grin_com

UNIVERSITY
of
ABERTAY DUNDEE

Foreign direct investments in Poland since 1989

Theoretical background, specific advantages and recent developments

Project Report for **EC 369A – Mini-Project on Europe**

in semester II of the academic year 2002/2003

at University of Abertay Dundee.

Date of submission: May 1st 2003

Michael A. Braun

Indexes

Table of contents

List of abbreviations

DC   developed country (ies)

ECE   east-central European country (ies)

e.g.   exempli gratia (lat.); for example

EMU   European Monetary Union

EU   European Union

FDI   foreign direct investment(s)

i.e.   id est (lat.); this means

ISA   internalisation-specific advantage(s)

LDC   less developed country (ies)

LSA   location-specific advantage(s)

MNC   multi-national company (ies)

NGO   non-governmental organisation(s)

OBM   obsolescing bargain model

OLI   paradigm of ownership, location and internalisation

OSA   ownership-specific advantage(s)

PI   portfolio investment

List of tables*   chapter

---

* All tables can be found in the appendix. The chapter tells the first naming of each table in the text.

1   Introduction and academic method

The collapse of communism has started a dramatic change in the economies and societies of eastern and central Europe (ECE). The transformation from a pre-planned to
a market-economic system has lead to the opening of previously shut markets. Since
1989 this region is not only a new market to sell to, but also a place to produce. And
especially western-European enterprises might benefit form this due to short distances, which help to integrate these locations into a worldwide firm-strategy.
European companies now have got the same possibilities like the US or even Japan to
produce cheaper directly at their doorstep. However, the integration of ECE does not
simply mean the extension of western markets to a eastern location. There is much
more such as the complete restructuring of western production chains. Or in other
words, there is a dual process of transformation (east) and structural change (west).
Therefore companies now have to ask themselves how to participate and benefit from
this challenge: Corporate investors face several options for expanding onto foreign
markets. There are such possibilities like exporting to these regions, licensing to local
partners, strategic alliances and joint ventures. But for several economic reasons, as
outlined in the next chapter, foreign direct investments (FDI) seem to be one of the
most common ways to go. But businesses also see, depending on contracts, the reduc-
tion of their own risk towards shared risk as a reasonable argument. Companies therefore are able to share their individual advantages and can concentrate on them. And
this is done quite often within recent history. [Deutsche Bank 2003, pp8]
In general it is interesting to look at the geographical spread of FDI streams. [Piggott
1999, pp258 / Deutsche Bank 2003, pp12] The majority of these investments
comes out of and also goes into the western hemisphere, but also to the south-eastern
parts of Asia. To a smaller extent FDI flows towards Latin America and the Carib-
bean. Africa is nearly not relevant when it comes to FDI transfers. Moreover, the DC
are not only responsible for most of the FDI, they are also investing it mostly in there
own rows. Also differences in sectors are various. Within DC services and high-tech
products dominate. While in LDC especially natural resources are involved.
Baring that in mind, this report focuses on Poland and its FDI inflows since 1989.
Therefore three questions can be asked now to concentrate on: (1) Why do companies
invest in general in foreign areas? (2) Why received this specific country capital from
international investors? And (3) finally, to what extent and in which sectors have foreign investors invested? Or, spoken more generally, this report will try to answer,
what the reasons are to invest in foreign countries and in particular why in Poland.
Thus all underlying research on this topic was done by the review of current literature
and the application of generally used economic theories. However, critical thinking in
combination with the use of common sense helped, too.
For a clear understanding, there will be two main chapters. One, which deals with the
theoretical background of FDI and political risk. Therefore some traditional and modern theories of FDI will be looked at more in depth. This is done basically from the
company's point of view (microeconomic perspective), rather than host country's
(macroeconomic perspective) one. However, the widely used concept (or paradigm)
of ownership, location and internalisation (OLI) is applied to the whole report. And as
a second major part of this chapter, the influence of political risk is assessed. For this
reason, the obsolescing barging model will be explained.
The other main chapter links these two parts with the FDI-region Poland. Thus, several authors argue, Poland is worth to invest in. This statement has to be looked at
more in depth to answer the underlying questions of this report. Therefore this chapter
is going to have a close look on specific reasons to invest in Poland. But also the FDI-

1

situation in Poland is part of the assessment. And in this chapter there are also figures provided on the Polish FDI-inflows since 1989.

FDI not always creates additional – obvious - value, apart from employment, for the host country. But often there are advantages of letting money into the country. For example the development from being a LDC towards a DC. This means the host country gains from specific advantages that come from outside (FDI investor). This topic will be looked at shortly as well. Moreover, afterwards a conclusion of the main findings combined with personal evaluations will be provided.

2 Theoretical background

2.1 Foreign direct investments

It seems that there is no general valid definition of FDI. But Piggott [1999, p255] define it 'as the acquisition, establishment, or increase in production facilities by a firm in a foreign country.' This means it has to be distinguished clearly to the sole credit-move of portfolio investment (PI). Whilst this means transfers to make profit, FDI as a production capital, a credit or even a mixed move of both is seeking for ownership and control over activities. But the process is more complex: it often does include not only financial involvement but also access to know-how and use of organisational and managerial abilities.

For a clear distinction FDI has to be divided into three parts: (1) Inflows, (2) outflows and (3) stock. The first one describes the amount of FDI received while the next means FDI, that went off the country. And finally stock is the total amount of all inward FDI undertaken yet. Since this report concentrates on FDI inflows, more comments can be made on this area: The certain country also has to be open in both ways – inward and outward - for capital flows. But its economy also should be attractive in general. [Zukrowska 2002, pp2]

Generally investor's reasons to do FDI are easily to understand. Often there is the argument investors want to gain form lower labour cost in foreign countries. But this is not always the case as FDI are undertaken mostly in DC. Also the share of labour cost compared to total cost declined over the last 50 years. [Piggott 1999, pp258 / Deutsche Bank 2003, pp12] But the cost for raw material, transport and power seem to be one key factor for investors. Therefore it can be regarded as more important, that high productivity, available knowledge and developed infrastructure are the stronger reasons for a investment-decision. Also access to resources, either human or natural, and local markets might be an argument. Moreover the overcome of barriers of entry and the diversification of the investing firm have to be taken into account as well. And a further explanation for FDI rather than another option are expected economies of scale. This means the average cost of production has an tendency to fall with an increase in size. Especially international specialisation can lead to dropping average costs through efficient resource allocation.

2.2 Paradigm of ownership, location and internalisation

The paradigm of OLI is a very general way to explain why enterprises undertake FDI. The following descriptions as well as the explanation of different FDI theories are based on Piggot [1999, pp260].

OLI names the three specific types of advantages, which are assumed to give MNC advantages. (1) Ownership-specific (OSA), (2) location-specific (LSA) and (3) internalisation-specific advantages (ISA).

The first one seems to be important when markets show some kind of imperfections. For example product differentiation, collusion and oligopoly. But these imperfections also may arise from economies of scale as well as due to governmental policies. Generally OSA can be divided into four main fields of advantages: Technical (e.g. patents, commercials secrets), industrial organization (e.g. economies of scale, joint R&D), financial and monetary (access to money) as well as access to raw materials. The second type of OLI advantages, LSA, deals with advantages that come up for companies form being located in a particular region. Not only access to the market and savings in transport cost but also in time are relevant for MNC. LSA as well can

be divided into four fields: access to raw materials, imperfections in international labour markets, trade barriers and government policies (e.g. taxation, regulation).
Finally the third type arises when imperfections make a market solution more costly
than a firm solution. Therefore the decision often is to carry out the task within the
company for a cheaper price. But to gain form this it is necessary to have the needed
materials and skills. If this is not the case, companies are able to internalise them from
another firm that has them already. And especially vertical integration leads to more
market power and assumable to more profit. But also the internalisation of specific
human skills and access to research activities make ISA attractive to foreign investors.

2.3   Traditional theories of foreign direct investments

Traditional theories of FDI are based on the neo-classical economic theory. They especially focus on LSA, while modern theories see the existence of imperfections in
markets either nationally or internationally. Therefore these theories suggest the arise
of considerable transaction costs for market solutions. But they also take managerial
and organisational functions into account as they are assumed to play a important role.
In the following, the most recognized traditional theory is looked at more in depth.

2.3.1   Capital arbitrage theory

Developed by Samuelson the capital arbitrage theory suggests that money is perfectly
mobile. This is valid not only nationally (across industries) but also internationally
(across borders). It flows form investments in either an industry or a country with low
return on investment to the ones with higher profits. And it does not matter whether
the theory is applied on PI or FDI – they flow both for the same reason the same way.
Reality, however, might be different: Some countries are both source of but also host
to FDI. This might be due to the fact that there are differences in the return on capital
between industries within a certain country. Further on, PI and FDI indeed do not always follow the same direction. The US for example is a net exporter of FDI but a net
importer of equity capital. [Dunning 1997, pp307]

2.4   Modern theories of foreign direct investments

2.4.1   Product-cycle model

This three-step-theory, based mainly on research about US FDI, was published by
Vernon in 1966. And especially two of the three OLI parts are seen to be important:
OSA and LSA. Theory suggested that 'new products' (step 1) first appear in the most
DC (and within the best companies) due to consumer demand. Later in order to be
profitable, 'maturing products' (step 2) become standardized and economies of scale
arise. Further on, while demand grows, prices decline and other advanced economies
start to become competitors. In this third step, the only criteria to sell 'standardized
products' is its price. Therefore firms have to search for the cheapest way to produce,
which leads them to LDC where labour cost is assumed to be lower than in DC.

2.4.2   Hymeranian view

Later Hymer argued in 1976 as well with an combination of OSA and LSA. The theory, which was, developed lines out that MNC gain advantage over local firms due to
imperfections in markets, e.g. technological progress. MNC were accused to invest
money in foreign markets to eliminate competition and to manipulate the market to-

wards an oligopolistic tendency. This should help them to become an even stronger
player in the market. But Hymer also had another explanation for FDI: money attracts
money, which basically means if one MNC in on a specific market, other competitors
will have to follow. The theory also prefers FDI to exports since these can be victims
of tariff barriers, further governmental policies and high transport costs. But FDI is
also preferred to franchising since of the arising lack of control. In general, Hymerian
view states that FDI is an instrument of showing power on oligopoly markets.

2.4.3 Internalisation theory

Coase developed the concept of internalisation in the 1930s but Buckley and Casson
were the first who linked ISA with theories of FDI. This is no surprise since the integration of R&D, production and marketing started to become crucial in the high-
technology era. Internalisation theory assumes imperfections in intermediate markets,
e.g. patented technological knowledge or specific human resources, which provide
great incentives to internalise them. And this leads MNC to buy-in these competitive
advantages – even in foreign countries. The authors show that incentives form internalisation depend on the interdependence between four main-factor groups: industry-,
region-, nation- and firm-specific incentives, which again are basically the assump-
tions of the OLI paradigm as well.

2.4.4 Eclectic theory

This theory combines the Hymerian view with the effects of internalisation as well. In
1981 Dunning added the three OLI parts together and developed the eclectic theory.
Basically it is argued that MNC need to have all the advantages to invest into foreign
countries. Firstly the question is why a company should invest there? Because of
LSA. For example: better access to markets. Secondly, how can MNC compete with
locals? Because of their OSA. This means e.g. the investing enterprise has got some
specific advantage. And finally, why do they use FDI instead of exporting or licensing? Because of ISA, which gives them account to all lacking resources. Political risk
Political risk is suggested to harm the profitability of a firm due to external (not intra-
industry) forces. [Moran 1999, pp15] This risk is different to commercial uncertain-
ties, acts of nature and accidents or theft. The next few paragraphs are based on
Moran [1999, pp15] and will outline political risk more clearly.

2.5 Political risk

2.5.1 Types of political risk

There are five main groups of such risk: (1) expropriation – nationalisation – confisca-
tion, (2) de facto expropriation, (3) currency risk, (4) risk of political violence and (5)
breach of contract. But nowadays several new kinds of political risk came up.
While in the first one the FDI host state takes over property of a MNC for diverse
reasons, either with or without payment of compensation, the second risk is a so
called 'domestication'. In this case increasing taxes or regulations as well as further
disadvantages make it much more difficult for firms to make money in this country.
The currency risk, which could be seen as an economic risk as well, is related to in-
convertibility of the foreign currency, changes of the exchange rate or inflation re-
spective devaluation due to massive printing of money. Even if an investor makes
profit in local currency, the company is not able to transfer it back home. Also exchange and price controls, tariffs and quotas as well as the current state of the econ-

omy are side effects of economic risk which influences the success of FDI. The forth group of risks deals with the classic kind of risk. E.g. war, civil war, revolution, terrorism, sabotage or movements towards independence. And finally breach of contract means the ex-ante change of agreements, which leads to a worse reputation of the particular country or even its government. Here the OBM helps to explain more. As a recent development new sources of risk came up: For example stronger local-business interests and decentralisation of power towards local councils compared to the government. But also pressure of NGO, intensive organised crime and corruption.

2.5.2 Obsolescing bargain model

Developed by Vernon [1971, pp21] the obsolescing bargain model (OBM) assumes that local investors are generally preferred to foreign ones. [Moran 1999, pp15] This applies especially in non-complete market economies. In addition, the model suggests there is some kind of bilateral monopoly between the host country and the investing firm. Before the contract is signed, uncertainty for the country is high. This is due to the fact, that the investor always can re-negotiate or change behaviour. Later, after the investment is done, the company has to bare the risk. The reason for this is that the behaviour of governments and local circumstances can change dramatically not to the favour of the investor. In the worst case, the mentioned types of risk apply.

However, Vernon [1971, pp56] continues to argue, investments shall be undertaken if the benefits outweigh the risk in terms of political and economical costs. The degree of risk depends on several aspects: First of all, OBM questions how long the investor is crucial for investment's success. This applies for example to the access to foreign markets (investors home market), to a continuing technology- or investment-transfer as well as to the amount of time that is needed to transfer the relevant knowledge. But also the kind of investment is interesting to look at within the OBM: If a company does a 'one-off' FDI (e.g. a oil-rig or a refinery), the risk included might be the highest due to the fact, that the investor is afterwards not necessary anymore. Therefore the government could tend to think about breaching contracts or confiscate investor's property. Moreover, a stable technology and undifferentiated products are seen to carry high risks on the long run for investors as well. Compared to this, a continuing flow of know-how such as in the high-tech industry protects against risk.

Additionally, potential competition with national or amongst other FDI investors within a certain country bares risk as well. A host country might try to protect own or certain companies against FDI-introduced competition. However, the amount of risk also depends, according to the OBM, on political sensitivity such as the quality of underlying relationships between host and source country and the prestige of the actual investment project. Finally, the calculated time that is available to generate profits determines the amount of risk, too. If a investor needs some time (high amount of capital or time-effects) to benefit from a investment, the risk might be higher also.

2.6 Conclusion of the theoretical part

To summarize the theoretical part it can be underlined, FDI is undertaken for several reasons. Therefore many authors have developed different models to explain theses reasons. But, generally spoken, they are always due to positive effects for companies. Otherwise a company might not want to undertake these actions anyway. Either these effects come from Samuelson's (capital arbitrage theory) or from Buckley and Casson's (internalisation theory) point of view, they are based on the OLI paradigm. Therefore this model is used in the next chapter to assess Poland's FDI-inflows since

1989. Additionally, at the influence of political risk in this period of time will be looked at a bit, too. For this reason, the OBM might help to evaluate.

3 Foreign direct investments location

3.1 Economic status

Poland nowadays is seen as a stable and reliable partner when it comes to a credit rating on a international basis. Thus, this country is rated number 37 from all states worldwide. [Anon. 2003a, p44] And even better: within the ECE-region, which consists of 25 states, Poland holds the forth place. [Anon. 2003a, p49] A low inflation rate (forecast 2003: 2,5%, one of the lowest in the ECE countries) and a increasingly stronger economical level (suggested for 2003 and 2004) that is above the EU-average support this point of view too. [Dresdner Bank 2003, p38 / Anon. 2003a, p49]The by far most important trade partners Poland's are its western neighbour-states. [Kurz 1998, pp48] And the percentage of exports that go to the European Union (EU) rose from 41,5% in 1989 up to 70,1% six years later. And especially Germany has got a major stake in this development. In 1995 in total 38,5% of their exports have gone to this country. Moreover, since Austrian firms often have got a German parent company, this figure even could be higher in reality. [Kurz 1998, p48] The same applies when it comes to imports into Poland. Here is Germany leader as well. Its stake was 26,6% in 1995.

3.2 Reasons for foreign direct investments in Poland

3.2.1 General method to assess a location

According to Zukrowska [2002, p6] investors are looking at external as well as internal conditions when planning to invest. This can be seen as well as an application of the L-part of the concept of OLI, too. External ones mean capital flows are secured by regional agreements such as a EU-membership or in the OECD. Moreover, there are global ones, too. For example being a member of GATT / WTO or having adapted IMF policies. Both do apply to Poland. Internal issues are all questions related to a specific location. Therefore a investor might look at labour and management issues. This includes e.g. the local cost of labour and working times, the level of education and qualification, productivity as well as the question of available suppliers. Further on, investors look at the market itself. Thus the size and growth of a certain market is relevant. Also questions related to customers (previous goods expenditures, income, etc.), competitors (barriers of entry, specific advantages, etc.) and the location are asked. Therefore infrastructure assets are suggested to be important. For example communication, transport, energy and the distance to existing plants and suppliers. Additionally, financial issues involve interest rates, inflation rates and the transfer of profits. This part especially is linked with all questions of political risk. Therefore tariffs and taxes but also the legal framework counts. Since Moran [1999, pp7] argues, political risk influences both financial and managerial questions of FDI, this topic seems to be relevant in particular. But also language barriers and the general the level of life is taken into consideration when it comes to invest in a foreign country.

3.2.2 Application of the OLI on Poland

As mentioned in the theoretical part previously, the OLI-paradigm consists of three areas to explain FDI. There are ownership-, location- and internalisation-specific advantages to take into consideration. Since ownership- and internalisation-specific advantages only can be investigated related to a certain case, this report focuses on loca-tion-specific advantages coming from a investment in Poland. And while Caétano [2002, p42] suggests, FDI are mainly driven by location-specific factors, this report is based on that assumption as well. Therefore the arguments that follow are closely linked with location-specific advantages.

Dunning [1997, pp210] points out; changes in the importance of a certain state within the international community can lead to an increase of FDI. But also the opening up of new territorial opportunities. Both, obviously, does apply to Poland. In 1989 the communism has collapsed. Thus, Poland was able to open up its market to foreign investments as well as for competition.

Since 1989 Poland has become a political and economical stable country. [Dresdner Bank 2003, p38] Additionally, the country is by far the biggest in terms of size and population amongst the enlargement-countries and it is in the geographical heart of Europe. [FAZ-Institute 2002, pp2] To make it clearer: Poland has got a bigger size and a amount of inhabitants than all other nine applicants together.

There is generally a investor-friendly legislation since FDI is regarded to be essential for the development and modernisation of the Polish economy. [Political risk services 2003, investment climate pp1] Foreign investors and companies are not discriminated, but they are treated similar to national ones. Property rights and investments are pro-tected and private business activities are forced. And the transfer of profits shall be possible without problems as well. The country has got a reasonable infrastructure and cultural support as well. [Kurz 1998, pp55] Poland has got a highly skilled workforce, but much cheaper labour costs. Therefore it is pointed out, [Kurz 1998, pp58] the main reason for investing in ECE is the 'least cost approach'. This means, corpora-tions are looking for the cheapest production opportunities. Which applies not only to ECE, but also to other FDI-locations worldwide. [Kynge 2002, p11]

There are close historical connections to the rest of Europe [Kurz 1998, pp45] over all periods within that last two thousand years. And according to many authors [e.g. Deutsche Bank 2003, p 29] Poland will probably join the EU in May 2004. But there-fore a poll has to be carried out before. Since the support in Poland's population for joining the EU is more than 50%, investors are not supposed to worried too much. [Polish embassy 2003, p1] Additionally the European Monetary Union (EMU) could be joined as well soon; some argue in 2007, some later. [Deutsche Bank 2003, p 29] Adaptation of the complete 'acquis communautaire' (EU-law) till 01.01.2005 is planned. [Polish embassy 2003, p3]

3.3 Flows of foreign direct investments into Poland

Poland has attracted a high level of FDI-capital in total since 1989. The reasons for choosing this location in particular to invest in has been various. As mentioned above, a large domestic market, a skilled work force and low labour cost were important. But also the relatively low level of risk, the distance to other plants within a worldwide production strategy and Poland's application to become a EU-member.

According to Zukrowska [2002, p9] Poland has received USD 9.3bn in 2000 and was therefore the biggest inflow-country in the ECE-region when it comes to FDI. This amount can be added to the high levels of FDI in previous years, too. See table 1. Nevertheless, Poland was not always the location that got most of the share. Between 1989 and 1995 Hungary has hold this position, handing it over since then to Poland. By the end of 2000 Poland has attracted more than USD 49bn cumulative FDI. See table 2. From this number, large investors (over USD 1m / project) have undertaken approx. 90%. [Political risk services 2003, investment climate p8] In total, 885 firms form 35 source locations have invested more than US 1m in this country

It might be interesting to look at the sources of FDI. Thus, France was the biggest investor by far in 2001. [Dresdner Bank 2002, p20] Companies from this country are responsible for about 33,8% of all FDI (2001: USD 6.7bn). Second was Germany being responsible for 19,2%. Followed by the US accounting for 9,7%. Statistics show as well, Belgium investors did 8,1% and British 5,9% of the FDI.

When one looks at the size of the individual projects, it has to be mentioned French investments were relatively large. [Political risk services 2003, investment climate p8] This is due to the total number of firms operating; France is only on third place having 70 companies investing in the country. Second is the US operating 130 and first Germany with 209 firms doing business. While this cannot be seen as the whole truth since some investing enterprises have got foreign parent companies but account for the subsidiary location rather then the origin of FDI-capital. For example Austrian suppliers that belong to German corporations. [Kurz 1998, p48]

The sectors to invest in are widespread. In total, the manufacturing sector seems to be the most popular since USD 19.5bn (39,4%) were invested between 1989 and 2000. [Political risk services 2003, investment climate p8] However, this applies not for every statistic in particular as banks and insurances were seen first by the FAZ-Institute [2002, p18] in 2001. See table 3. They are followed by the retail and repair (USD 6,1bn, 11,4%) and transport and communications (USD 5,7bn, 10,7%) This might be caused due to a different distinction between several sectors. Additionally Dresdner Bank [2002, p20] sees food in front (33,2%) followed by production (23,5%) and retail and finance.

Over all, the four main types of FDI [Dunning 1997, pp219] can be found over the period of time. There are investors operating that are resource seeking, market seeking, efficiency seeking and strategic asset seeking. And indeed many of the investors are doing a strategy that changes by time. [Kurz 1998, pp56] But they are all seen as being close in line to the optimal management strategy. [Caétano 2002, p36]

3.4 Effects of foreign direct investments

3.4.1 On the source country

Capital transfers lead to different results in the source as well as in the host country. But generally, most economists argue, according to Zukrowska [2002, pp2], source countries benefit more.

Since money flows out of one to another economy, the outflow state looses capital for consumption. However, due to the individual decision to save and invest the money rather then to consume, this would not be a problem. Nevertheless, less capital in one economy might lead to higher interest rates, which could harm the home economy. Overall it can be theoretically argued with Samuleson's capital arbitrage theory. Money that flows from one economic location, where profits are relatively low to another place, where they are higher, generates a better turnover and leads to a more efficient allocation of scarce resources. [Pigott 1999, pp254]

And probably one the most important changes in recent years has been the emergence of a real global economy and the structural integration of markets and production systems. [Dunning 1997, pp226] Therefore Kurz [1998, pp61] points out, a strategy of complementing specialization and integration can be found often. In the beginning of such a investment process, companies are often looking for lower costs (least cost approach). But later, after they gained trust, they change their attitude towards more independent foreign plants, which are important in a international corporate system.

3.4.2 On the host country

According to Caétano [2002, p32] FDI are seen as the fastest way to transfer a market economic culture to a former centralized and planned economy. This seems to apply especially for the ECE countries and in particular Poland.

But host countries also seek for more than a transformation of their market. According to Blomström [2000, pp101] the main reason for them might be to acquire modern technology in combination with production, management and marketing knowledge. Even a investor runs a project fully on his own, the knowledge will flow into to country anyway since it is some kind of a public good. [Blomström 2000, pp101] These kinds of effects are often referred as 'productivity spillovers'.

Other positive externalities would be forward or backward linkages with the investing company but also a increasing competition. In addition, 'market access spillovers' due to a specific knowledge in how to enter foreign markets might flow into as well. Also a change from a receiver of FDI to a exporter is possible and can be observed recently. [Kynge 2002, p11] This as well goes in line with a change from a sole production to a research and development location. [Kurz 1998, pp63]

4   Conclusion

As outlined in the introduction, the collapse of communism has started a dramatic change in the economies and societies of eastern and central Europe (ECE). And especially western-European firms can benefit form this due to short distances, which help to integrate these locations into a worldwide firm-strategy.

This report was going to show the inflows of FDI into Poland. Thus a core model was used: the concept of ownership-, location- and internalisation-specific advantages.

For several economic reasons, as outlined in the previous chapters, foreign direct investments (FDI) seem to be a common way to expand onto foreign markets. Therefore, three questions were being asked to concentrate on: (1) Why do companies invest in general in foreign areas? (2) Why received Poland in particular capital from international investors? And (3) finally, to what extent and in which sectors have foreign investors invested?

The first question was answered by arguing ownership-, location- and internalisation-specific advantages (OLI-paradigm) apply and make investors to invest abroad rather than at home. This assumption was supported as well by Samuelson's capital arbitrage theory. Continuing, the question arose why foreign companies especially invest in Poland. Therefore mainly location-specific advantages such as a EU-membership in future, the short distance to the western-European production plants and a highly skilled and cheap workforce were seen as main reasons. And the last question was to what extent firms have invested in the country. Therefore it was argued, Poland is the biggest FDI inflow-country amongst all the enlargement-candidates. Even this applied only since 1995; Poland has shown stability and got investor's trust.

One does not know what future might bring. But for sure can be, Poland has tried to find its position recently within a new world order. After centuries of not being independent, this county now seems to be willing to search for a stable and peaceful future. Therefore FDI are seen by many authors to help to stabilize and to develop that country. And even the short period of time since 1989 might underline this, too.

Appendix

Table 1

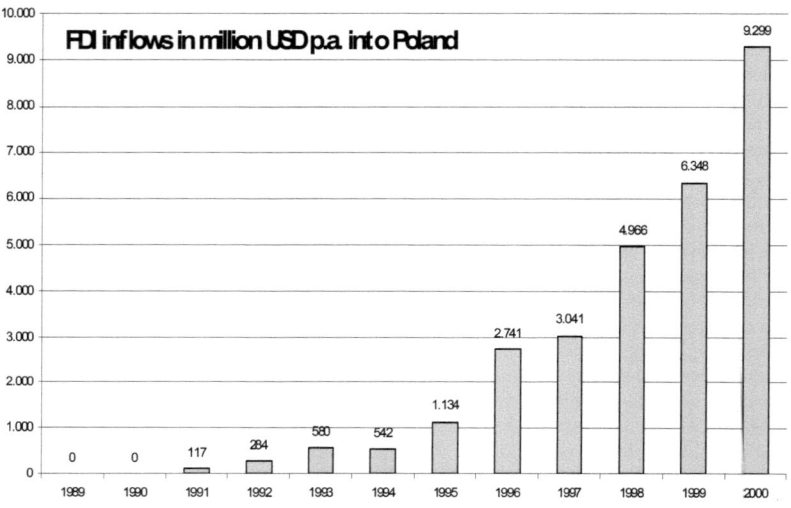

Source: Ezoneplus working paper no. 7a, p9

Table 2

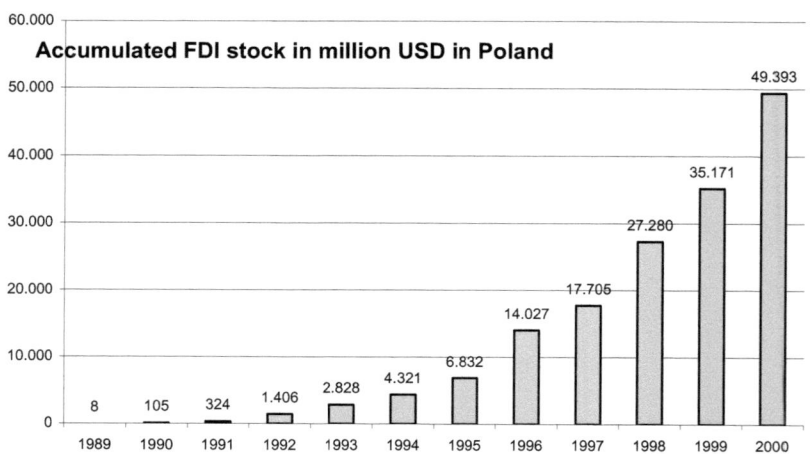

Source: Ezoneplus working paper no. 7a, p19

Table 3

Main sectors of FDI inflows into Poland

Sector	Invested capital (end 2001, in bn USD)	Part of all FDI
Banks, insurances	12,3	23,1%
Retail, repair	6,1	11,4%
Transport, communications	5,7	10,7%
Food, agriculture	5,5	10,4%
Automotive, suppliers	5,4	10,2%
Others	18,2	34,3%
Sum	53,2	100,0%

Source: FAZ-Institute 2002, p38

List of references

Books

Blomström, M., Kokko, A. and Zejan, M. 2000. *Foreign direct investments*. London: MacMillan Press

Dunning, J. 1997. *Alliance capitalism and global business*. London: Routledge

Moran, Th. ed. 1999. *Managing international political risk*. Harlow: Longman

Piggott, J., Cook, M. 1999. *International business economics*. 2nd edition. Harlow: Longman

Vernon, R. 1971. *Sovereignty at bay: Multinational spread of US enterprise*. New York: Basic Books

Journals and newspapers

Anon. 2003a. Institutional Investor's 2003 country credit ratings. *Institutional Investor*. Issue 03: pp 44

Anon. 2003b. Infineon Asia Pacific - Singapore's many faces. *Infineon Galaxy*. Issue 03/2003: pp16

Kynge, J. 2002. Doing overtime in the workshop of the world. *Financial Times*. 29. October: p11

Discussion papers and studies

Caétano, J. et al. 2002. *Ezoneplus working paper no. 7 - The eastward enlargement of the Eurozone*. [online] Berlin: Jean Monnet Centre of Excellence. Available from: http://www.ezoneplus.org/publications.php [Accessed 21 February 2003]

Deutsche Bank. 2003. *Mittel- & Osteuropa – Konvergenz*. London: Research-Büro Deutsche Bank

Dresdner Bank. 2003. Polen: Politische Unsicherheit. *Wirtschaft International*. Issue 05/2003: pp18

Dresdner Bank. 2002. *Investieren in Mittel- und Osteuropa*. Frankfurt: Dresdner Bank

FAZ-Institute. 2002. *Länderanalyse Polen – November 2000*. Frankfurt am Main: F.A.Z.-Institute

Kurz, C. and Wittke, V. 1998. Die Nutzung industrieller Kapazitäten in Mitteleuropa durch westliche Unternehmen. *SOFI-Mitteilungen*. Issue 26/98: pp45

Political risk services. 2003. *Poland – Country forecast*. Location unknown: political risk service

Zukrowska, K. et al. 2002. *Ezoneplus working paper no. 7a - Exemplification of Poland and other post-communist states*. [online] Berlin: Jean Monnet Centre of Excellence. Available from: http://www.ezoneplus.org/publications.php [Accessed 21 February 2003]

Internet sources

Polish Embassy. 2003. *Polens Wirtschaft und die polnisch-deutschen Wirtschaftsbeziehungen im Jahre 2001*. [online] Berlin, Polish Embassy. Available from: http://www.wirtschaft-polen.de/de/index.php3 [Accessed 03 March 2003]